Freedom seekers

Kerry Needs

Create a life that works for you

Table of Contents

Why I Wrote this book

'Don't ask yourself what the world needs. Ask yourself what makes you come alive, and then go out and do that, because what the world needs is people who have come alive' - Howard Thurman

At twenty years old, I was just about to leave University, having gained a first class honours in Communication Studies. I was seeing a careers counsellor in my final year, and a book in her office gleamed and caught my eye. It was called 'The Career Guide for Creative and Unconventional People.' Something about that spoke to me at just twenty years old. What was 'unconventional?' I wondered.

Fast forward 13 years, and I've definitely not taken the well-trodden path when it comes to work. I have tried over fifty different jobs in my life, looking for ones that suit my personality, interests, and where I feel I can really make a valuable difference.

I have:

- Completed a PG Certificate in Consciousness and Transpersonal Psychology at Liverpool John Moores University

- Run my own online magazine on mind-body medicine and consciousness

- Practised as a hypnotherapist, seeing clients at a therapy centre

- Waitressed

- Worked in retail

- Worked as a children's entertainer, dressing up as a Disney princess

- Worked for a film production company as a production assistant

- Worked as a Fitness instructor at aerobics classes

- Worked for an administrator for a charity

- Worked as a careers counsellor at a university

- Worked in marketing as a content manager

- Worked for a language school taking students out on day trips around the UK

- Freelanced in copywriting, brand strategy and marketing

Pretty unconventional, don't you think? After a while, I realised that the way most of our work life is set up denies our own personal autonomy, freedom and individual creativity (unless of course, you're your own boss). You might get one of those in a 'regular' employed job, but you'd be hard pushed to get all three.

I wanted to design my own life - I didn't want to give a huge portion of my time away to an employer purely for the sake of a salary.

This was my life, after all, and it's really precious. So I've been freedom seeking ever since, and found a variety of ways to live an unconventional, alternative lifestyle that allows for a more fluid, flowing life - free of the rigid confines of a structured working week.

This path is not for everyone; so I won't be offended if right now, you put this book down.

But if you're just a *teeny bit* intrigued at exploring another possibility, then read on...

Where you might be now

Are you a victim of 'the cultural system'?

> *"Most people are other people. Their thoughts are someone else's opinions, their lives a mimicry, their passions a quotation." - Oscar Wilde*

Firstly let me explain what I mean about 'the cultural system'. The system as I define it is the grid lines that have been paved by the majority of society and are perpetuated by the mainstream media.

This cultural system essentially defines what 'normal' is, and as 'normal' is ever changing, then what rings true now may not be the case in 5-10 years time. Things are evolving really, really fast.

For the purposes of this book, which is aimed at the western worker, let's say if you're 'in the system', this probably rings true:

- You work at a job which defines your working hours

- You travel to a place of work, called your commute

- Your main time off is at weekends, or booked annual leave (maximum four weeks a year)

- In your lifetime, the amount of time you personally control is less than what your organisation controls

- You are saving for retirement, a large block of time nearer to the end of your life

The average person spends **90,000 hours** at work over their lifetime. That's roughly 10 solid years of never ending work. Phew.

There are some patterns we have fallen into in the West that have made us unhealthy. Stress is the leading cause of ill health at work, and 1 in 4 adults has some form of anxiety or depression. That makes me really sad. We're not looking after ourselves as well as we could be. Perhaps we need a bit of a detox from our current system?

Should you 'detox' from this system?

Well, the only reason we ever detox from anything is when we've overdone it, and it's causing a detriment to us in some way.

Only you know if you'd like to detox the system, but here are a few clues:

- More often than not, you're stressed

- More often than not, you're tired

- More often than not, you're overwhelmed

- More often than not, you're frustrated

- More often than not, you're doing things you'd rather not do

- More often than not, you feel like you haven't got enough time

These are signals to us that somewhere, the scales have tipped out of balance. A life out of balance doesn't feel very good at all, whereas if you start to take these toxic elements out of your life, you'll find that you begin to feel healthier and happier, as you put all aspects of your life to work.

The war on your mind

'We're living at a time when attention is the new currency' - Pete Cashmore

There's a fierce war going on, much more prevalent than anything the world has ever seen before. But this war is not one that can be seen too easily. It's an invisible war; a war of thoughts. There are millions of people battling for the most precious thing from you every day - your attention.

The war is a war on your mind. We are bombarded everyday with millions of messages from the media, all telling us how we should live our lives.

Sometimes people want our attention to sell us something, sometimes they want to push an agenda, or sometimes they want to give us information. Being aware of what we've been paying attention to can make all the difference.

Fear is a powerful attention magnet.

When you're in fear, you can be easily controlled.

The person who fears getting the sack will do everything to ensure they look good in their boss's eyes.

The person who fears being rejected will do everything in their power to appease their partner.

The person who fears death clings to life and is scared to step out of their comfort zone.

I actually heard a story recently about a man that is so fearful about having enough money for his retirement that he has £4 million saved, and that's still 'not enough'.

To me, and to probably most other humans in the world, that is insane.

We are incredibly, incredibly rich in the West. We unfortunately have been conditioned to believe in scarcity, in lack, and in fear, and it is this mindset that I wish to detox you from.

My inner mindset mantra was:

'It's so hard to survive; I'm on this financial treadmill forever, and I'm trapped in a job that doesn't fulfil me. I'm not feeling inspired or energised, and I have to do this for the rest of my life?'

As I got older, it got harder. Once I got past my twenties, I noticed everyone had already started or rapidly started to stockpile money - we weren't allowed to be carefree anymore, we had to be 'sensible'. We had to think about mortgages, and pensions, and ISAs, and of course insurance, and family planning, and maybe investing… it was all too much for me, and just made the weight of earning money even greater.

I wanted to set my own rules. As long as I was making money, then it didn't matter how, right?

If you feel the same, and are ready for a new way of thinking, then let's get started.

Disclaimer: You have to really want it

Before I begin, I need to warn you.

This is not an easy path by all means; in fact, it is far, far easier to stick to what you know. It is easier to stay within the confines of a 9-5, earn a regular salary, and stick within the comfortable bubble of your own comfort zone. It's easy to do what everyone else is doing.

But you don't want that anymore, right? You long for more meaning in your life. You want more time, more freedom.

There's no mistaking it - modern life can be *tough*. And it's primarily tough because there's so many frickin things to do. Most of us have a commute to do, have car insurance to pay, need time to organise our hair appointments, spend our weekend or lunch break buying a present for a friend's new baby, spend our evening calling a plumber to look at your boiler…. The list goes on, and can be endless.

'Life admin' as I like to call it, can get overwhelming, especially if you've got a full time job and responsibilities. Our minds and bodies rarely get a respite from the pace of modern life, and it is this that leads us to feel stuck, frustrated, and maybe even depressed.

Freedom seeking is primarily about slowing down. It's about seeking more of a balance between doing and *being*.

If you've picked up this book, you'd like to spend time reading, looking at the stars, playing in the sea, discovering new places and lands and people - in short; you want to live more.

You want to feel the feeling of being fully *alive*. You know that the meaning of your existence is not just to grow up, have a family, pay bills, and die. You're worth more.

You're looking for a life beyond ordinary. You know it exists, but you just need help getting there.

Above all, you really, really want it. You don't want to waste a single second more dreaming about what could be, instead of taking action.

You, my dear, may well be a Freedom Seeker.

Why be a freedom seeker?

'Do not go where the path may lead; go where there is no path, and lead a trail' - Ralph Waldo Emerson

Not that I really need to convince you, because you're reading this book. But here's just some of the things you *could* get by having more control over your working week:

Travel - No more two week holidays, now you can travel for as long as you like! After a day by the pool, you can bring your laptop and soak up the sun as you earn your money. Bliss!

More exercise - Fed up of all those people in the pool during your morning swim? Well don't worry any more, because you might be able to do your swim at 2pm on a Tuesday afternoon, when it's blissfully quiet. Hurrah!

Vitamin D - If it's blazing hot outside, and you want to take a two hour lunch to sunbathe, who cares? You're a freedom seeker, and you work when you choose. Heck, if you wanted to sun worship all day, and work all night, that's totally up to you.

No commute - Never again shall you have your face pressed up against someone else's stinking pits on the Tube. (Unless of course you want to, you know, whatever floats your boat.)

Less pollution - If you are being flexible with your work life, chances are you'll work from home from time to time. So by using your car a little less, you're even helping the environment a little less. Yay!

More time for housework- Saturdays don't need to be wasted cleaning or doing piles of washing. Nope, you can do a little bit every day! It's a good way to take a break from your computer, having a bit of a hoover and a boogie.

No office politics - No office life means no office politics, but it also means no camaraderie. Boohoo. Oh, unless you get yourself to one of the THOUSANDS of coworking spaces, all over the world. Have a little Google, I'm sure there is a coworking space near you where you'll meet loads of other people in the same boat as you. More fun, less politics.

Appointments galore - Now this was a biggie for me, because at one point not only did I used to have a plethora of doctors and hospital appointments, I also had things like hair appointments, acupuncture, nail appointments. How is a girl to fit all of those things into her life without taking holiday? You might say. Now you can organise your schedule to suit you. Result = instant happiness.

Family time - You want to spend a Friday taking your little ones to the zoo? You want your dad to pop over for a cuppa in between work? No problem. You'll be able to have more time for the people you love, and not just try and squeeze them all in your already over-full diary.

Earn more - With remote work, for the first time in history, you're not limited to earning in your own country and currency. If you're in a country that has a weak currency, you can really boost your income by getting a remote job or by freelancing in other countries.

More energy - Now this is not guaranteed, because you might decide you want to become the world's richest person in the whole world and be literally glued to your computer morning, noon, and night… but my love, that's not what freedom seeking is all about. With all the above benefits, you naturally should have more energy.

Maybe you actually like your 9-5 job, and love working in an office. That's great! Or perhaps you enjoy office life, but just want a bit more flexibility.

Flexible working can have it's benefits too, because even though you have to work a set amount of hours per week, it's absolutely up to you which ones you choose to work. This can help relieve mental stress and pressure. It can also help you take those baby steps towards true freedom.

Are you a freedom seeker?

> *'All good things are wild and free.' - Henry David Thoreau*

I've always been a freedom seeker. I love feeling totally free, open to where life takes me, and on an ever-expanding quest of learning, knowledge and growth.

Wanting to feel more free is natural. It's about wanting to be in control of your time, of your life, of setting up the life you've always wanted. Believe it or not; it's easier than you think to do.

Freedom seekers are growing in the world. There's more people that are taking their wealth, their health, and their happiness into their own hands, and feeling empowered.

Here's how you can spot one:

Freedom seekers share knowledge

If you're a freedom seeker, you love knowledge, but you also love to share it. You realise knowledge is power. When I was writing this book, I was at a hostel in Lisbon, chilling out on their rooftop terrace. A guy came over to chat, and after some brief conversation he told me that he is sick of the 9-5, and wants to live life on his own terms. I then passionately told him all the tips I knew of that could help him on his journey.

My mantra, when it comes to someone making a big or scary life change, that they know inside will make them happier, is 'DO IT!' It's better to have tried and failed than have not tried at all.

I'm a bit of a knowledge recycler. I guzzle it, absorb it, and then regurgitate it. It was only after many years of posting things like 'This video is amazing!' on Twitter, or 'Such an interesting article!' on Linkedin, that I knew my ability to absorb and share information was a skill that could be used to help other people escape their current situation.

Knowledge is, after all, power.

Freedom seekers love to travel

Even if you've got responsibilities, if you're a freedom seeker, you love to travel. You are at your most alive when you're in a new place, seeking out new cultures, new tastes and sights, and you adore meeting new people (that's the knowledge thing).

One of the main reasons people want to escape the 9-5 and live more freely is so they can travel, but for you it might be different. It may be that you want more time to spend with your children, or to care for an elderly relative.

Either way, to you, having more control over your own time (therefore your life), means the world to you, and being more free has become one of your most highest values.

Freedom seekers are continually focused on growth

If you're a freedom seeker, you continually seek growth and expansion. You love improving yourself and making yourself better, whether that's in the area of your career, health, relationships, spirituality, family, or just all around.

You might feel frustrated that you don't have enough time to dedicate yourself to the hobbies and the interests that matter to you; and that has enabled you to seek out alternative ways of living.

Freedom seekers make up their own mind

You know your own mind. You're strong. You're courageous. And even if you are absolutely terrified of making a freedom seeking decision, the fact that you're reading information about it shows you are committed to yourself enough to at least explore the option.

You may weigh up options carefully, or you may dive straight in - but your motivation is the same. You don't want to 'play it too safe' anymore. You realise that life is too short.

You know that having possessions and material things are of little value compared to time, health and experiences. Those things really matter to you - having the time to spend with loved ones, getting your health in fantastic condition, and having the freedom to really enjoy your life and have some amazing experiences.

You don't always follow the crowd or believe what you read in the media. You think 'well, that's just what they think!' You're independent, and a 'big-picture' thinker; you see your life holistically.

Even though your family, your partner, your friends and the media have an influence on you, you ultimately come to your own conclusions, based upon your lived experience.

What's your definition of success?

'Success is liking yourself, liking what you do,
and liking how you do it' - Maya Angelou

To get from where we are, we need to know where we're going, right? I encourage you to look at your freedom seeking in a way that looks at every aspect of your life, not just your career.

I largely feel 'outside the system'. I don't sit in traffic or get crushed in a commute, I don't 'live for the weekend', I don't clock watch, I don't sit in meetings, feeling utterly frustrated that I'm wasting my life, and it feels SO GOOD.

My definition of success was to be able to spend my life in

my own way, to be as free as possible from the 'should's' of society (fuck the 'shoulds, right?)

Success is being redefined by those who are no longer a slave to the corporate 'system'.

Success is now being defined by how much time you have, by how much control you have over your time, and ultimately, how happy you are.

Is the man who works 90 hours a week, earns £200,000 a year, but barely sees his friends and family more successful than the mum who has set up a laptop lifestyle, and manages to travel, and spend more time looking after her children?

I've realised that each person's definition of success is different - there's no one size fits all.

If you want to be a surfer dude in Thailand, chilling by day, and working by night, then who is anyone to say you should be doing anything else?

It's about defining what makes you happy.

Sometimes, this is actually difficult, because we've been so conditioned by the system to believe that we want or need certain things, that we don't actually check in with ourselves to see what makes ourselves happy.

For a lot of people, it's not just about 'werk werk werk', it's also about having time to do hobbies. Maybe you want to learn a new language, maybe you'd like to spend more time cooking healthier meals, maybe you'd like to write a book.

Sound too good to be true? That's just 'system thinking'.

So let's start our first detox - removing those 'should' toxins out of your mindset, and figuring out how you'd truly love to spend your time.

- When do you feel most alive?

____

____

____

____

- When do you feel time slips away?

____

____

____

____

- If you were to die within a year, what would you like to do?

____

____

____

____

- What appeals to you most about being free from the system?

____

____

____

What is 'rich', anyway?

Are you rich?

What is your first answer to that question? I bet you're thinking in terms of money, aren't you? Well as the granddaddy of remote work Timothy Ferris (author of the 4 hour work week) states, there is something called the 'New Rich.'

These people are time rich. They may also be cash rich, but primarily they have the choice to spend their lives in the way that they want.

Are you rich in health?

Are you rich in friends, family and connections?

Are you rich in wanting to improve your mind and body?

Yes? Then maybe it's time you redefined what rich means to you.

I am incredibly rich, but I never felt it in the past because I was always focusing on one tiny aspect - money. Having money does definitely not make you a rich person. You can have money and be lonely, have money and be an alcoholic, or have money and be stressed all the time.

Being rich is about two things - happiness and health.

The two are actually mutually exclusive; you can't have one without the other, really.

The way to cultivate these is by realising where you already have them in your life.

The more you focus on your happiness and wellbeing, the easier it will be to adjust your internal definition of what 'rich' looks like, and it will be easier for you to attract money because you're not making it your sole focus.

There's a couple of ways you can instantly feel richer - and it takes just a few simple minutes each day.

The first is what I call a 'gratitude tree'. Draw a tree, and write your name on the trunk. On the branches, write down all the good things you have in your life - names of people, your nice house, the lovely walk to your local park, your cat - it can be literally anything.

At the end of every day or every week, update your tree with more branches and leaves. It could be a new skill you've learned, a new person you've met, or a new savings goal you've reached. You will see your gratitude tree bloom before your eyes, and realise just how much goodness exists in your world.

Another exercise is what I have termed 'feel good things that have happened this year'. Get a glass jar, stick a smiley face on it, and get some pen and paper. Every time something happens that makes you laugh, or you have a fun experience, write it down. You can save them up for a whole year, or do a 'feel good jar' each week

It will make you feel great when you re-read all the great experiences and memories you've been making. Sometimes we just need to be reminded of all the good we have in order to feel truly rich.

What specifically do you want?

> *'Your vision will only become clear when you look into your heart. Who looks outside, dreams, but who looks inside, awakens' - Carl Jung*

It's important to get really clear about what you want, because what you think you want may not be the right thing for you.

Sit with yourself for a while; say 30 minutes. No distractions. No phone, no TV, no computer, no people, no noise.

Just you and your idea.

Think about what you need most right now. Is it a new experience, rest, development, adventure, meeting new contacts?

It's all about what you would like to experience.

For example, I had a desire to spend a month with an off grid community, learning the methods they used, and generally just learning from them, and how they 'do' life. It became apparent that if I stayed as a volunteer and helped them for 5 hours a day, I wouldn't be able to do my remote work (or I would, but I'd be at my computer for several hours a day, and pretty much miss everything).

After much trying to make it work, and figuring it out, I realised I needed experiences where I took a solid break away from my computer, perhaps doing 1-2 hours a day online. I wanted experiences where I could primarily be 100% present in the moment, and my energy wasn't split.

By that I mean that my thoughts weren't in two places - I could be fully attentive to what was going on around me. After all, this is the delicious, juicy part of the travel experience - the rich feast it offers for your senses.

I decided to continue with freelancing and remote working but also look for occasional contracting work - which usually paid a high day rate, allowing me to save a large chunk of money in a short space of time. It suited my fast work ethic, and also my ability to get bored easily (*hey, I've only got 6 weeks in this place left!*)

What's more, it allowed me to really be specific about the experiences I wanted, and of course to change things if I needed to.

I began to dream things like:

- Going on a month long yoga retreat

- Staying in an off grid community

- Working on an organic farm

- Doing a clean water project

- Volunteering in an orphanage

- Completing an Asian cookery course

- Doing a conservation project

- Hanging out in Bali for a month

- Going on a writing retreat

- Completing a meditation course

When I really got specific, I realised that the reason I wanted to be a remote worker is because I wanted these experiences. I didn't necessarily want to be working 24/7, I also wanted the freedom to connect with others.

This feeling of community and connection is what I carried with me, and it allowed me to direct my attention in the right way, and have clear goals as a remote worker.

I can now honestly say that every year I have a new experience where I am growing, as this is really important to me. It is my highest value in life, spiritual growth.

But this may be your idea of hell. That's not your path; it's cool. You have to work out what matters to you, what lights you up, and makes your eyes sparkle.

To get specific, keep asking yourself 'why?'

I know you want this life, but 'why?'

'Why that?'

'Why?'

'Why?'

And so on, until you find the answer.

Do you believe it's possible?

Belief is the fuel needed to get you up the mountain. With belief, you can scale to amazing heights.

If you lack belief in yourself, it's going to be a great deal harder to create the life you want. So if you've been telling yourself it's just 'too difficult', then STOP today!

Creating a more freedom based lifestyle starts with the belief that it's possible.

We have our beliefs already ingrained in us from childhood, or from our peers, so if we are feeling stuck it may just be that we have surrounded ourselves with limited thinkers.

To start to free yourself, you must first free your mind. If you ask it 'Why am I stuck?' It will give you an answer. If you start asking it better questions, it has to give you better results.

Start small, and make a plan.

What do you need to learn to make this happen? Is it a new skill, a contact, or a new job?

How can you meet people that may be interested in creating a similar lifestyle?

When you're around people that have similar desires and enthusiasm for a particular lifestyle, amazing things can happen.

If you're not, it's going to be a lot harder to get the energetic fuel needed to make a change.

Anywhere you are, there are going to be people that have similar interests as you. You just have to find them. Even if you think it's going to be a needle in the haystack.

If you're surrounded by people that think your dream is impossible, or at the very least impossible for them, it might make it more difficult for you to make the leap.

In reality, our possibilities are endless, it's only our beliefs that hold us back from making them come true.

Making the decision

Detoxing your thinking

Before I start, I need to warn you what this detox is all about. It's a super fresh, nutrient rich dose of self-love.

So if there's anything that you currently put above yourself, like other people's demands or money or recognition, now is the time to stop.

I realised that when I was miserable and frustrated at work, it was because I wasn't giving myself permission to make a change. You're the result of your decisions, right?

So even if you have a family, and a mortgage, and 'not enough time', there will still be a way you can set up your life so you become a little more free.

And it starts with your thinking.

You see, there are all things in life that we are told we 'should' do, when in fact, the choice is ours to make. It's naturally assumed that most of us will go to college, get a full time job, get a mortgage, have a pension. But in reality, you don't have to do any of those things.

Some of the most successful people, who are living a life of freedom, haven't always done things the conventional way.

Forming new beliefs

'It is better to be hated for who you are, than loved for who you are not' - Andre Gide

There's certain beliefs we may have adopted about this lifestyle from society, our parents, or the media, and to be honest, they're not very helpful. They can keep us stuck, miserable and depressed.

It's so weird isn't it, that something invisible and intangible can keep us in a prison of our own making.

What do I mean? Well, beliefs like this:

'I'm xx. I should have found my career by now'
'I can't break up with them; it won't look good to my parents'
'Travelling's for youngsters; not someone like me'
'I should be settling down by now'
'I'm too old for that'
'It's not really what I should be doing'

You can see that there's a whole lotta unhelpful thinking in there, right?

One of the only reasons why you're not where you want to be is because you might have some limiting beliefs that are holding you back.

The beliefs you have are yours to change. If they're not serving you right now, why not make them into something more positive?

The thing is, our beliefs usually run on autopilot. They run our lives, because they tell our minds what's important.

If we tell our minds, hang on a minute, I'm not going to believe that any more, it will of course ignore you at first. But if you consistently form new beliefs that are the opposite of the ones you've been believing in, you'll start to turn things around and orientate yourself into a new direction. We need to start telling ourselves a new *story,* and give our feelings a different meaning.

Those people who talk down to you because you are daring to try something new are those who don't have the balls to do it themselves.

Go ahead. Let them judge you.

Where there's a will, there's a way

'But I have a life and responsibilities… how can I 'be free'?'

It's a question I have heard before.

I can guarantee you that it's possible that you can be *more free* than you are now.

Sometimes, moving our life in a different direction requires a different way of thinking. Where there is a will, there is a way

But I have children?

If you have children, a combination of income streams may work best for you, as you may want to work at various times, and when you choose. Sites such as Cloud Peeps (www.

cloudpeeps.com) and Upwork (www.upwork.com) may offer you some income, and you could even decide to sell products, such as becoming a Partylite (www.Partylite.co.uk) or Neals Yard Consultant.

But I have a mortgage?

You can start your life to freedom by getting a remote job, as I did. Working remotely gives you the opportunity to try out this lifestyle for yourself, to see if you like it. With a remote job, your mortgage will be covered and it will free up your time and energy to follow more creative pursuits, if you so choose.

But I can't do my profession online?

… Think again! Even if you're a hairdresser, there are a ton of ways you can set up your life to be a little bit freer. For example, you could create a series of Udemy (www.udemy.com) courses on cutting hair, or become a dropshipper for hair products. That way you keep your profession, but it doesn't have to consume your life and your time, because you have other income streams.

Smashing through the fear

'Your greatest gift lies behind a door named fear' - Sufis

To take action towards what you want, you really need to stare your fears in the face.

Most of our fears are really fears of the unknown. We've never been in this situation before; what if we can't handle it?

I know lots about fear; because I consistently identified with it. All those little 'what if's?' in your mind when you do a scary thing never stopped me from taking action, but I took action anyway, but still *identified with and focused on the fear.*

This is where I went wrong. I was so afraid of ending up broke, ending up sick, that I literally pulled those things into existence for myself, because I could not see any other possibility.

I wasn't prepared for either of those things, and caused myself stress.

I now know that with a fear, you just have to know that focusing on your worries won't help. Sure, make adequate adjustments to your life to make sure you have a safety net, but don't focus so exclusively on falling.

The Sufi's once said:

'Your greatest gift lies behind a door named fear' ; and I believe this is absolutely true.

However, we can view our fears in a different way - by seeing them as opportunities to believe in ourselves more.

What fears do you have about living a life on your own terms?

____

____

____

____

____

____

____

How can these be turned into opportunities? For each fear you wrote down, write down a different way of looking at the situation, or taking another course of action:

____

____

____

____

____

____

Some of the most common fears I'll list below; and a way for you to overcome them:

'I won't be able to pay the bills'

- Starting this lifestyle is not about going off and quitting your job tomorrow, and then figuring out a plan (trust me I've done that and it's not recommended!) Start with a plan of 3-6 months, or longer if that suits you. It could be starting a sideline service whilst you're at your full time job, or looking for a remote job first, whilst you build up freelancing or other sources of income. Where there is a will, there is almost certainly a way.

'What will my boss/parents/spouse/friends think?'

- To be truly free, we need to be free of what other people think of us. This can be hard, but once we have our plan set in our own mind, it will be easier to remain strong in our decision and happy with the choice we have made. Only you know how unhappy you have been in your current situation; and only you have to live with the consequences of not exploring this opportunity for freedom. If another also wants happiness and freedom for you, they will support your decision. Just don't let their fears become your own.

'What if I'm isolated or lonely?'

- Whatever your reason for wanting to manage your own time; the paradox is that you become 100% responsible for your life. You are in greater control of your freedom; so whatever you choose is yours! If you want to spend your days at home with your children, working in between being a parent, that's great. If you want to take your laptop on adventures and travel the world, that's great too. Being isolated or lonely can only occur if you don't make the most of the current opportunities available to you. Make a list of all the ways you could meet people as a freedom seeker.

Playing it safe vs being free

You probably know someone in your life who has always played it safe. Doesn't like to take risks, stays with the things they know, and does all things possible to avoid change.

This person's highest value is safety. They are likely to be careful with money, they weigh things up carefully, and usually uses logic to make decisions in their life.

You may also know someone who is a risk taker. These people enjoy adventure, like things to be constantly changing, and don't enjoy routine.

This person's highest value is freedom. They are likely to value experiences over money, make quick decisions, and follow their heart and emotions when deciding on a course of action.

I'm here to say; it's not an either/or situation.

You don't have to be a) a person who plays it safe or b) a person who craves freedom. You can have both.

All of us want safety, and all of us want freedom, and it's very possible to have both. You don't need to choose between: a) living the corporate life and climbing the housing ladder, and b) wandering the world barefoot with a bunch of hippies. It's ok, I understand that either one may be a bit too extreme for you - a happy medium is fine.

The thing is, in any situation, it's never black and white; it's usually both/and. The incredibly 'safe player' always secretly wants to take a risk, but is frightened, and the incredibly 'risky player' has a deep need for stability but sometimes it isn't there. If it is, then great! That's what we're aiming for.

But because we don't see it as a both/and situation, we sometimes berate each other's life choices when we're on the other side of the fence:

'They're living recklessly!'
'They're boring!'

The truth is, it's all about balance, of course. And it's about happiness. What is boring to you may not be boring to someone else. What seems reckless to you may feel absolutely normal to someone else.

There might be some scared little voices in the back of your mind when it comes to living this way.

What are they saying?
How are you holding yourself back?

Are you worried about your stability, or are you frightened of freedom?

Write down all those thoughts here.

____

____

____

____

____

____

The hardest part of being a freedom seeker

Now, when you read this title, what did you think? I'm guessing you thought the hardest part was going to be the fear of what other people think, or money, or acquiring knowledge or skills to take your life in a different direction.

Nope.

The hardest part of being a freedom seeker is making a choice to commit yourself to freedom.

The hardest part is recognising that freedom is one of your highest values, and you thoroughly deserve to be happy.

The hardest part is *being honest with yourself.* It's hard making that decision at the deepest core of your being, and then being courageous enough to follow through with that - no matter what.

You know before you go on a scary ride at a theme park or you do something shit-scary you've never done before?

Usually, the fear is greatest *before* you step onto the ride - it's your thoughts themselves that are making this whole experience poop your pants scary.

It's ok to take your time to make this decision. It is, after all a big one. But don't get paralysed by fear, like I did.

I spent four years with a strong dream and desire within me, but I was absolutely terrified of breaking out of the norm and going for it. Even though, in the last two years, I'd nearly died twice.

I had a huge HGV lorry slam into the back of my car on the M6, writing it off, and nearly writing me off in the process.

A couple of years later, I went to Bali on what was supposed to be a month long restful break, only to find myself progressively paralysed with some (still unknown) illness, and being airlifted on a private jet to a hospital in Singapore. I was in a wheelchair for about three weeks.

Both TERRIFYING experiences.

Even the more terrifying because it seemed like they were little wake up calls, little nudges from the universe, saying to me 'Erm, Kerry, haven't you always followed your heart? Haven't you always been courageous? Why are you denying your own truths and accepting a life experience that is not fulfilling your soul?

So, yeah, the universe got me on that one.

Taking on a new mindset

The most powerful tool at your disposal

*'The mind is it's own place and can make a
heaven of hell, a hell of heaven' - John Milton*

One of the most powerful tools I used for the creation of
the life I wanted to lead is something invisible. It's actually
weightless, too, and I carry it around with me all the time, so I
can use it whenever I want. The most difficult thing is actually
remembering to use it!

It's my imagination - one of the most underrated tools we all
have at our disposal.

Even if you feel a million miles away from where you want to
be, you have your imagination. You have your mindset, and
you have the power of visualisation.

I cannot underestimate how important and valuable this tool
is. You actually require far less effort than you think you do,
once your mind and emotions are correctly aligned towards
what you wish to become.

Using your imagination is something that can be incorporated into your everyday life, as it doesn't take effort, just commitment.

It of course has to be coupled with action; but the action can be taken in a gentle, happy and relaxed way, rather than a fearful and stressful way. You're not going to get great results if you stress too much about not having it.

By using the power of your mind and visualisation, you'll not only feel more empowered, but you're orientating yourself towards your dreams, and away from your fears.

The power of the mind is incredible; but it is only incredible if we know how powerful it is. And the only way we know how powerful it is, is to test it out in our own experience. Each and every day, staying faithful to the dream within you, with a happy heart and a relaxed attitude about it.

Sound difficult? It's not. Just like going to the gym, the more you utilise this power, the stronger it will be.

Here's how you get started. You define what your vision would look like, in crystal clear detail, and then you utilise all of your senses in your imagination.

I will know I have achieved my freedom seeking dream by the fact that:

____

____

____

____

____

Once I have achieved this, the things I would see around me are:

____

____

____

____

____

Once I have achieved this, I'd have so much more of this in my life:

____

____

____

____

____

Once I have achieved this, this is how it would feel inside:

____

____

____

____

____

Once I have achieved this, this is how I would look to other people:

____

____

____

____

____

You've got some answers written down, right? This will form the basis of your *dream vision.* Everyday, you can go into your dream vision - the most powerful time to do it is when you're falling asleep at night.

You must stick to your vision though, and hold the feelings within you on a consistent basis. Not only will it make you feel good, but it will stop you from thinking negatively about the situation - you are imbuing your mind with positive energy. This will give you the motivation and energy to do what you need to do everyday.

By all means, I know what happens if you focus on the opposite. If all you are doing is internally saying to yourself 'I'm stuck' or 'I'm trapped', then all you will do is replicate your experiences. You're talking down to yourself in your mind, and that is not a good place to start from, because the now is all we have, and in the now, all possibility is contained.

So forget what's happened up to this point and *know* that you can create a freedom seeking life for yourself, you just have to want it bad enough that you'll commit yourself to it everyday, and really revel in those lovely emotions you're feeling as you visualise your success.

Every choice you make counts

The decisions that have the most beneficial impact on our lives are not necessarily the easiest choices to make. In fact, they are usually some of the hardest choices we will ever make.

Taking the decision to get up early and search for remote jobs is not an easy decision, but it's one that will get you to where you want to be.

Making a decision that you will eat healthier foods and spend more time cooking is not an easy choice to make after a tiring and stressful day, but it's one that is aligned with your values.

Taking action to structure your time and say no to commitments may not be an easy decision if you're a people pleaser, but it will give you the necessary energy needed in order to commit to yourself.

You want to make a change. If you didn't, you wouldn't be reading this, right?

I was only able to write this book when I realised that I had to *choose* to write, every single day, even when I didn't feel like it, because if I waited until I 'had the spare time' or 'when I felt like it', well, you and I know, this book wasn't going to be written.

It's sometimes really hard to push yourself to be committed and to discipline yourself towards any particular goal. Especially if you've had a lifetime of talking yourself out of things.

The only thing that actually really motivates me to do anything like this is the fact that I might die tomorrow. No, seriously - if you live with death in mind then you're not going to keep procrastinating and putting stuff off, are you?

Let's think about your freer lifestyle for a second.

Really envisage what that looks like; in minute detail.

Are you spending more time at the gym?

More time travelling, perhaps working in beautiful coworking spots?

Are you working in the morning and then having the afternoons off with your family?

Are you spending more time at home, trying out new recipes?

Are you having lie-ins, and doing the bulk of your work in the evening?

Whatever freedom-seeking life looks like to you, imagine that in crystal clear detail. Make it so real and vivid in your mind, and feel those feelings as if you're living that life now - abundant, healthy, happy and free. Maybe even write down your ideal day, from start to finish.

Feel good?

Now, whenever you feel the urge to slack off and not commit yourself to this goal, I want you to think about three things -

a.) **This vision**

b.) **If you died before achieving this vision**

c.) **If you died having achieved this vision**

It may sound morbid, but death is a bloody good motivator. We haven't all got access to a little 'Grim Reaper' clock that tells us how long we have left, so think about how you'd like to spend your time left here.

Fill out the following:

At the end of my life, I'd be proud of myself if I:

____

____

____

____

Now write out that sentence and stick it where you can see it ;)

Expanding time

> *'Your time is limited, so don't waste it living someone else's life' - Steve Jobs*

One of the best things being more free and in control of your work life gives you is greater control over your time.

As I say this, I have just got up at my usual time of 6am (ugh!) to write this book. I get up, pour myself a cup of tea, sit in my dressing gown, open my laptop, start writing, and don't stop until I've reached my 500 word target.

When I was working for someone else it would be hard to do this, for a few reasons:

- I would probably have to get ready soon and start my commute and the thought of this may stress me out. It would be playing on my mind.

- In my full time job I would usually have had a huge demanding workload, and be more stressed

- I would be forced to sit at a computer for a further 9 hours a day, even if I didn't feel like it

Sound familiar?

In fact, those reasons were the reason I became a freedom seeker, particularly the last one.

When I worked in an office doing a 9-5 job, I seriously struggled. I work quite fast, and sometimes I'd have a super productive day, burning through tons of tasks, and then by

2:30/3pm, I'd be ready to go home. I would have exhausted all of my mental energy, yet I still had 2 hours, sometimes 3, before I was allowed to go home.

This to me was absolutely soul destroying. I knew I had done great work; I knew I had achieved in 6 hours what a lot of people achieve in 8, but yet I had to sit here, pretending to look busy for the next two hours, or finding myself jobs to do that I really didn't have the energy for.

The biggest problem for me was not actually having the time - it was not having the energy.

Without energy, we can't create. We can't think up new solutions. We can't take ourselves in a different path. We just end up feeling 'stuck', tired, and frustrated.

I've lost count of the amount of times I've been sad at a desk for thinking that thought. All I could think is 'I want my freedom!' and since I've had it, I'm so grateful that I don't feel like that anymore.

You can too.

When time becomes your own, it can become your friend instead of your enemy. You can meld into it, flow with it, instead of watching it miserably.

How do you do this?

By filling your life with things that really mean something to you.

Sure, money is important, but so are memories that you've enjoyed something in your day - time out for a nap, for meditation, to catch up with a friend, or to try a new recipe.

Let's get thinking about your time. What would you do if you had more control over it, and the energy to spend it in the way you want?

If I had more time and energy, I would:

____

____

____

____

____

If I had more time and energy, I would:

____

____

____

____

____

If I had more time and energy, I would:

____

____

____

____

____

The most valuable currency we all have is time itself. It is a gift we have, we don't know how long we have got, and we can spend it in whatever way we choose.

Some of us waste it, some of us save it, but one things for sure - we never know just how precious it is until we have very little of it left.

Time is the most valuable thing we have. Every day is an opportunity to use what we have, love and appreciate each day, and make valuable changes to our lives.

If there's one thing I have learned, it is never ever too late to do what you'd love to do. Even if you are 90 years old. Time can shackle us sometimes, because we get caught up in what we 'should' be doing at our age, but it doesn't have to.

Time is the only currency we have that we spend, and we can never get back. What will you do with your daily 86,400 seconds?

What I learned on my journey

What I've learned so far on this journey

So being a freedom seeker, you'll know that you love to share and spread the knowledge love, and that is certainly true of myself. I get excited when I find other people's views that are similar to mine (I'm not so different in wanting this lifestyle after all!)

Reading and learning enables you to find the fuel and motivation to push for more. It enables you to learn from others, integrate their wisdom with your own experience, and set bigger goals for your freedom-seeking life.

Here's the most inspiring books, blogs, and resources that helped me. I hope it helps you too.

Books

Screw Work, Let's Play

I loved the title of this, and the book didn't disappoint. It's not a 'pie in the sky' book, but is filled with both inspirational and practical steps to doing your first 'Play Project'; and taking the steps to filling your time with things you actually enjoy doing.

Free Range Human, by Marianne Cantwell

I adore this book. It inspires me greatly; because Marianne talks to you like her very best friend; one she cares about, and really wants to help. If you're in need of extra motivation to live this lifestyle; buy this book. You won't regret it.

You are a BadAss, by Jen Sincero

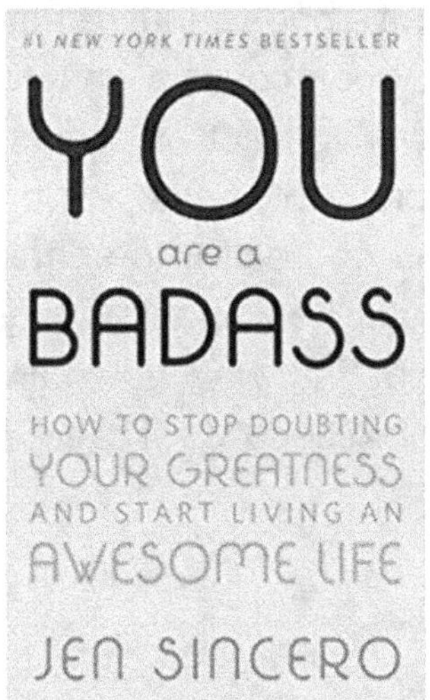

I actually haven't read this book; I just listened to the audio version. And I love it! Jen speaks with such power and personality that it's like your very own pep talk. Everyone needs a mentor, and Jen fiercely encourages you to be your best self.

The Art of Non Conformity, by Chris Guillebeau

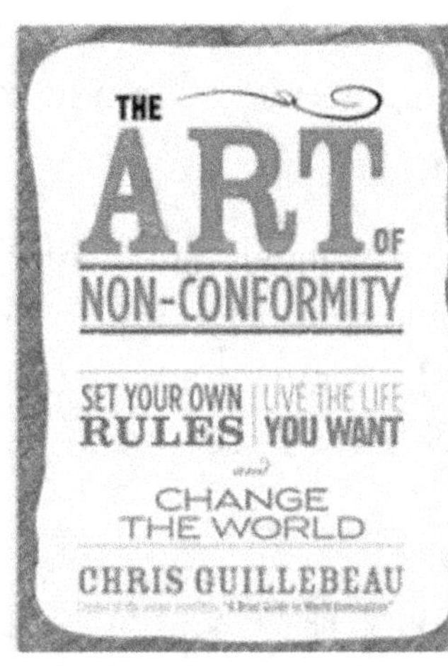

This book may not be for everyone; it packs quite a punch. That said, if you're in dire need of some motivation and feel stuck in a rut, then there's no better book. Chris speaks authentically and openly on why so many people aren't living their best lives, and this book is as scary as it is exciting. Once you've read it, you'll never be the same again.

Mindset, by Carol Dweck

Mindset is not a book about remote work, but it does cover a chapter on business. In fact, it covers every topic of life, from relationships, to health, to sports. It's a fantastic book packed with evidence that the way you think makes *all* the difference. Try it.

Social Media

Facebook Groups

When I started a laptop lifestyle, I knew there were hundreds of thousands of opportunities out there; you just needed to know where to look.

Part of the difficulty people have when transitioning to this kind of lifestyle is that they simply don't have the time to do the reading and researching - it's hard to know where to look, and that in itself can mean you're stuck where you are for far longer than you need to be.

Here's some of the groups I've found. I don't like Facebook, but I find it useful to meet people who are working remotely. The groups below have been *invaluable* on my journey - there's so many questions people have, and everyone answers them for each other - it's really nice. On some of these groups, there are plenty of job opportunities too!

Group: Digital Nomads Remote Work - Telecommuters
Group: Digital Nomad: Remote Job Opportunities
Group: DNX Digital Nomads and Lifehacker Community
Group: Digital Nomads around the World
(Ladies only) Group: Digital Nomads Girls Community

Online Resources

No Desk (www.nodesk.co) is a fab website that pretty much covers you with all the remote work basics - coworking, travel, books, jobs - all on one site! Check them out if you ever need inspiration.

Nomadlist (www.nomadlist.com) Pieter Levels has created many sites for nomads, and Nomad List is a great tool to see which countries are great to work on.

Youtubers

These Youtubers are people that discuss some of the topics in this book. Their content is focused on living freely, abundance, travelling, digital nomadism, and building income streams. There are so many out there; it's best to watch a view and find a person that resonates with you.

Zoey Arielle - Zoe has a huge amount of travel videos, but there are a few little nuggets on digital nomadism. Zoe has set up a freedom seeker lifestyle and is living in Italy.

Digital Nomad Girl - This lovely lady has some really helpful advice in terms of helping others to become location independent and has lots of very practical tips.

Your new life

Building multiple income streams

Believe it or not, there are TONS of ways to make money online. Some I haven't even heard of, and new ways are springing up all the time.

It's a really exciting time!

Here's everything I can think of at the moment to make money online (2017)

- Freelancing sites

- A remote job

- Making a course

- Being a Youtuber with ads

- Creating a Patreon account

- Using a Crowdfunding platform

- User testing

- Selling a product or service online

- Dropshipping

- Affiliate marketing

- Investing

- Teach English online

- Coaching online

- Virtual Assistant (VA)

- Translator

- Trend Forecasting

The general consensus is that you need a few income streams rather than just one, so you're effectively financially covered if anything happens.

The portfolio career

> *'No problem can be solved from the same level of consciousness that created it' - Albert Einstein*

When it comes to creating a more freedom-based lifestyle, we need to start thinking outside the box. Traditionally, we had one to three jobs throughout our lifetime; but this has now changed. Jobs are more accessible and more transient than ever before.

What this means is that you don't even need to stick to one job. Try on the 'portfolio career' for size.

A portfolio career is where you make a living doing several things; indulging your skills and passions, but having a varied lifestyle.

If you're a multi-passionate person, and enjoy many different hobbies and learning new skills, this could be the right move for you.

For example:

- You could work part time as a marketing manager, and teach yoga.

- You could start a dropshipping business and also childmind in your free time.

- You could be an IT programmer, and also write online courses.

- You could be an online recruiter, and also have your own dog walking business.

A portfolio career is the answer to today's modern 'gig economy', where jobs of under two years are seen as normal.

Having a portfolio career can be a good idea in an unstable economy, as you maximise your sources of income.

I've always struggled to title myself when it comes to a biography or 'About me' section on social media. I mean, I'm a lot of things! It's really hard to pin it down to just one.

For example, I

- Write books

- Make videos

- Do freelance consulting

- Own a website on consciousness

- Co-run a philosophy group

- Enjoy dancing and performing speeches and workshops

There are drawbacks to a portfolio career though, such as managing your time. But if you crave variety, and above all autonomy for your life, this path may be the right one for you.

It's a way you can design your own life.

A lot of people who have a portfolio career use one job as an 'anchor', as their main source. This may or may not be a remote job; but it will free up time for you to either pursue an alternative career, build up a stream of income, or explore ways to make money online.

If you're thinking about a portfolio career, list out your main skills and qualities that people would pay for. Are you a great communicator? Do you have experience and contacts in a particular field?

If you combine your skills with a variety of jobs, it can make you feel more confident, as well as increasing your social skills and ability to form new friendships and contacts. You never know who you might meet!

Build your ideal portfolio career below - what would you do if you could do a mix of anything?

____

____

____

____

____

Want a new career direction?

If you'd like to just earn money online but haven't got many skills, You can start with admin jobs such as a VA (Virtual Assistant), online customer service jobs such as those with Salesforce (www.salesforce.com), or take a TEFL (Teach English as a Foreign Language) and teach english online.

What is passive income?

Passive income is basically making money whilst you do *nada*.

It's not totally passive, though, because there's usually a huge investment of time in creating the stream before you let it loose into the world.

A passive income stream could be a book, a course, an app - anything that requires creation and then people can just buy it.

It's not all plain sailing, though.

Of course, you still need a good marketing plan, but if you do your research and create something people want, at the right time (my friend Joe struck gold with his hypnotherapy downloads), then you're going to really free your time up.

Passive income can snowball quite easily; so if you have a great product that is packaged well, the rest should take care of itself.

I don't claim to be an expert on this subject, but it is certainly an area of income I think most of us should be looking into, especially as passive income can provide us a little nest egg as we approach old age and retirement.

Job sites

Working remotely is essentially having a full time job, but instead of being at an office, you can work from anywhere. This gives you the security of a regular salary, but without the commute.

There are new ones springing up all the time; social media is a good place to find them (do a keyword search in the search bar), but here's a list of 20 helpful websites to get you started.

1. We Work Remotely (www.weworkremotely.com)

2. Remote.ok.io (www.remoteok.io)

3. Working Nomads (www.workingnomads.co)

4. Remoters (www.remoters.net)

5. The Gig Economist (www.gigeconomist.co.uk)

6. Problogger (www.problogger.com/jobs)

7. Skip the Drive (www.skipthedrive.com)

8. Flexjobs (www.flexjobs.com)

9. AngelList (www.angel.co)

10. Remote Work Hub (www.remoteworkhub.com)

11. Escape the City (www.escapethecity.org)

12. Jobpresso (www.jobpresso.co)

13. WFH.io (www.wfh.io)

14. No Desk. co (www.nodesk.co)

15. Work in Startups (www.workinstartups.com)

16. Power to Fly (www.powertofly.com)

17. Indeed.co.uk (www.indeed.co.uk)

18. Remotive (www.remotive.io)

19. Outsourcely (www.outsourcely.com)

20. The Muse (www.themuse.com)

Freelancing Sites

On a freelance site, you can offer your skills and get paid - it's as simple as that.

Whether you're a writer, a coder, a graphic designer, an accountant or a teacher - there's a whole host of sites out there to pay you.

It's not easy though. Don't expect to apply for a few and expect the money to come rolling in instantly. It takes work. But if you're committed, here's a few sites to get you started:

1. Upwork (www.upwork.com)

2. Fiverr (www.fiverr.com)

3. People Per Hour (www.peopleperhour.com)

4. Cloud Peeps (www.cloudpeeps.com)

5. Freelancer (www.freelancer.com)

6. Flexjobs (www.flexjobs.com)

7. Hubstaff (www.hubstaff.com)

8. Guru (www.guru.com)

9. Craigslist (www.craiglist.org)

10. Contently (www.contently.com/jobs)

Content Creating

If you love being in front of a camera, making videos, then becoming a content creator may be the right step for you.

Content creation can be anything, from creating videos, to books, to podcasts. It takes work though, because to build a following in content, you need to be creating on a consistent basis.

If Youtube or Podcasting is your thing, Patreon (www.patreon.com) is a great place to get sponsored. Patreon is essentially a crowdfunding site, whereby people will sponsor you to generate content.

If you have just a 1,000 paying members, you can be well on your way to funding a lifestyle as a content creator.

Product creation

Sites such as Kickstarter (www.kickstarter.com), Crowdfunder (www.crowdfunder.co.uk), and IndieGogo (www.indiegogo.com) can help you crowdfund a product such as a book, an app, or a new business idea. You can create a product page, set a target for fundraising, and then spread the word far and wide!

The key here is not just to build a great product. It's to build something that is unique enough and has a certain demand, even if that demand is just 1,000 people. There are a huge amount of books, apps and products out there - how will you make yours stand out from the crowd?

Etsy (www.etsy.com), Amazon (www.amazon.com) or Ebay (www.ebay.com) are great ways to sell products online.

There's really a lot of ways you could sell something - think creatively!

Have a think about how you could sell your skills online. You can sell practically anything online now.

You don't just need to sell physical products, though.

For example, if you're a photographer, you can sell your photography on places like IstockPhoto (www.istockphoto.com).

Explore the world

Travel

I went to a great little social enterprise cafe in Shoreditch called The Canvas Cafe, which allows visitors to write on their walls about their dreams, hopes, memories and fears. In answer to the question 'Where would you like to be in 10 years?' The number one reason people on that wall involved travel.

'Travelling the world' is high on many people's lists, because it offers so many things. It offers exploration, knowledge, exposure to other countries, a sense of awe, and a feeling of freedom.

It's not always rainbows and roses, though, of course. Travelling can be seriously shitty at times (literally), when you're holed up with some illness and missing your family and you're in a noisy room with a hard bed and can't sleep.

I personally think the good aspects of travelling far outweigh the bad, though. Even before I became location independent I have had the travel bug. I blame my mum for taking me on the Inca trail when I was 21.

Affording travel

Although I have always earned a low to average salary, I have always rearranged my life so I could travel. I've been to quite a few countries; but my list of places to see grows rather than shrinks!

So many people think travel is expensive; but it's really not, if travel is your number one priority in life. If your number one priority is comfort, or style, then yes, it can get expensive.

Even when I have been making less than £25,000 a year, I have still prioritised travel and allowed myself to travel. It involves me making other sacrifices in my life, but those to me are worth it.

- **Transport** - I don't have a fancy car. Nor did I pay for it on credit; I bought what many would consider an 'old banger' outright. As I work from home or on the move, I don't use it for long distances that often, and because it's a cheap car, it's very affordable to fill up.

- **Clothes** - I buy lots of my clothes from charity and vintage shops. At first I felt a bit weird doing so, but after a while I actually liked it. It takes a bit more hunting and searching for the right pieces, but it's guilt free shopping - every piece I buy helps others!

- **House** - I have mainly lived in rented accommodation, and currently don't have a mortgage (although I could if I wanted to). Buying property is a cultural thing, and really depends on where you live. In some countries people don't buy houses at all, and that is totally normal. But this is not for everyone - you've got to do what makes you feel comfortable.

- **Socialising** - This is actually where I do spend money. In fact, I live like a traveller most of the time if I think about it, I cook quite a bit wherever I'm staying and enjoy it, but I do enjoy going out - eating at restaurants, going to networking and social events, going to the cinema. It gives my life variety, so I wouldn't want to stop that.

- **Objects** - I don't have much stuff. I buy very little furniture (the pieces I do have I would be happy to store), and I do a clear out every few months. The things I do keep are memorabilia - my dance trophy from a friends wedding, photos, old diaries, and books. I basically just keep physical representations of memories.

- **Money** - I have a pension, I have savings, and I have insurance for important things in my life. Since I know what it is like to be totally broke, and I also know what it is like to be very ill, I think these two things are absolutely vital to protect if you want to live a life of freedom. Protect your money, and protect your health. I would strongly advise to get health insurance for peace of mind. I'm thankful I had it when I got ill in Bali. If I hadn't, I would have faced bills of over £50,000.

- **Food -** For household food and other items, I set a strict budget, and get my food shopping delivered. I then just buy the essentials without being tempted to throw things in my basket at a supermarket (besides which, I absolutely detest grocery shopping and find it much easier to do online). Of course, you can't always have your food shopping delivered when you're on your travels, so I stick to a budget, and have 1-2 days a week where I eat very plain, simple and cheap foods, so I can splash out on other days.

Setting up an escape plan

A life on the road is not always easy, and most people don't pursue this for various reasons. I personally prefer to travel slowly, and enjoy holidays and short breaks being location independent.

There are various things to consider when travelling; I don't claim to be an expert on this section of the book, but here's just a few things to consider:

Before leaving the country:

- **Phone**

You'll probably want to get an unlocked phone with a SIM you can use abroad, but if you're travelling in Europe remember that as of 2017 the laws have changed, so you can use your free minutes and data without being charged (unless you go over your allowance, of course). Always check the latest forums - I find the Digital Nomad Facebook groups mentioned in this book a good source of information.

- **Storage**

You can rent storage space for £10 a week or less; it's pretty easy to do, and there are lots out there. If you haven't got space of your own to store stuff, ask favours of friends or family before renting storage space. However, storage space is insured, so if the worst happens, you should be covered.

- **Medical Insurance**

This is a biggie. As you know, I have witnessed first hand what happens when you fall seriously ill abroad and need urgent medical assistance with the help of insurers. If you're already protected, check the small print. Most insurers only cover you for a certain amount of time, but you can be insured for longer with companies such as World Nomads (www.worldnomads. com). Ensure you also have any relevant vaccinations before you go.

- Mail

It's easy to manage your mail whilst you're away, too. You can buy a virtual postbox from places like Mail Box Etc (www.mbe. com), or even get a service that opens and scans your mail for you, like Traveling Mailbox.

- Visa

Before you travel, check the conditions of the country, and how long you can stay for. It's wise to make a diary note of when you should expect to apply for a visa, and leave a bit of contingency room in case things are slower than you might want.

- Travel gear

I like to travel light, usually taking carry on luggage (a small rucksack and a short suitcase for small trips, or a backpack for longer trips). What you find now with most airlines is that your laptop will have to be scanned separately, and usually placed in the cabin with you, as so to avoid damage. You can buy Eagle Creek's (www.eaglecreek.com) compression packing cubes to help you.

After you fly

- Getting around

Buying a small rucksack to put my laptop in was one of the best decisions I have made. Years ago, I still used to carry a laptop bag around with me, and not only did it look horribly briefcase looking; it screamed *'I'm carrying a laptop- somebody mug me!'* Thankfully I didn't get mugged, but always felt wary carrying it around. It also meant I only had one hand to open doors, etc.

- **Being safe**

Being safe is just a matter of attitude as it is learning about where you're going. Do some research on places to avoid, and make sure that if you're on your own, you're not going anywhere too deserted at night. Don't draw attention to yourself as a tourist by pulling your map out on busy street corners; find a cafe instead. Similarly, wait until you're in a quiet place to count your money. Finally, let other people back home know where you'll be from time to time, so they are able to reach you should they need to.

Meeting other Freedom Seekers

Meetup.com

I set up my own Digital Nomads meetup in Nottingham when I arrived; I met a few people from it that were living in a different way, but there wasn't a huge amount of those kind of people to sustain the group and for it to grow, so I handed it over.

Check out the meetups (www.meetup.com) in your area; and when you're travelling, do a little search on Meetup to find people. You won't be lonely, because they're always there; you just need to know where to look!

For example, Lisbon Digital Nomads is a thriving group; attracting people from all over the globe to their regular socials, with a usual attendance of over 70.

Hobbies

A great way to meet likeminded people is simply to do the hobbies you've done back at home. Search for yoga or cookery classes, take a hiking or walking tour - whatever takes your fancy! Meeting people this way ensures you have something in common with them, and allows for a more bonding experience.

Accommodation

Housesitting

Housesitting can be a really cheap and cost effective way to save money whilst on the road. I've never done it, but sites such as Trusted Housesitters (www.trustedhousesitters.com) means that if you have pets, someone will come and look after them for free for you, whilst they get a free stay out of the deal.

There's also sites like Nomador (www.nomador.com) where you can browse hundreds of travel destinations, and find the house that's right for you. If you're looking to save money whilst travelling, housesitting may be a good option.

Airbnb

You've probably all heard of Airbnb (www.airbnb.co.uk) - a great and cheap way to find local accommodation. I've used it both as a host and as a guest.

But there are alternatives to airbnb; try Couchsurfing (www. couchsurfing.com), or Wimdu (www.wimdu.com), or do a google search for 'Alternatives to Airbnb'. There's lots out there, you just have to look!

Hostels

Love them or hate them; hostels are here to stay. I actually enjoy hostels (for the most part), as usually when I stay I'm looking for the social aspect of meeting new people and having a laugh. If comfort and peace are your top priorities, you're probably better off in a hotel, but having said that, hostels do sometimes offer private rooms, so you can get the best of both worlds. Try Hostel World (www.hostelworld.com) for some top tips, or just do a search on best hostels in that area.

Coliving

Coliving is a new concept; taking the hostel model one step further for us freedom seekers. It essentially combines those who live a laptop lifestyle with some sweet accommodation, enabling you to meet others in the same boat. Although not always glossy and glamorous, these do have a higher price tag than other accommodation options. Check out Roam (www.roam.co) with spots in Bali, Miami, London, and Tokyo, or other spots like Outsite (www.outsite.co) I've no doubt this is an area which will massively grow over the next few years as the scene develops.

Travel programmes

These are programmes where you travel with a group of individuals to further enrich your travel experience. This could be short stints, for a month (like Unsettled www.beunsettled. co) or something a bit longer term, like Remote Year (www. remoteyear.com), where you and over others could be travelling the world for up to 12 months.

Intentional (eco) communities

Intentional communities are purposeful communities that get together and live in a particular space with the intention of living off the land. Some of these are off grid, but communities with access to wifi, such as Merkaba (www.merkabacommunity. com) in Portugal allow the individual to take part in a truly life-transforming experience. It may not be your cup of tea, but if you fancy unplugging for a while and living as close to nature as you can get, then it may be worth giving it a whirl.

Volunteering

If you find yourself with more time on your hands and less work to do; then volunteering can be a great way to experience something new. Sites such as WWOOF (www. wwoofinternational.org) and Workaway (www.workaway. info) can give you a really different experience, in which you'll usually be working from 4-6 hours a day, with a couple of days off in the week. If you choose a place with wifi, you'll still be able to keep things ticking over should you need to. Volunteering is also a great chance to meet people from other cultures.

Your new workspaces

__Workspace__

Choosing your workspace is really important. For the first time, we have the power to decide! No more stuffy office cubicles, we can work however we want!

Here's some options for a freedom seeking work lifestyle. They're not for everyone, so test each one out until you find the combination that's right for you.

Coworking spaces

You've probably heard of the term 'coworking spaces'. If you haven't, it's essentially this: a room or a space used as an office, with a load of freelancers working from it. It's not hot desking because the focus is on the community; and quite often, you can buy access to your own desk. Traditionally, the only office option for freelancers and remote workers was a random office desk in a building full of businesses.

The world is changing in the freedom seekers favour (hurrah!) and this means that there are more and more spaces catered to and tailored for the freelancer.

Coworking spaces can be a good idea for remote workers

because it provides that all important community aspect. (There's only so long you can continue to talk to the cat, right?).

Benefits of coworking spaces

Like anything, the proof is in the pudding. Don't take my word for it.

Coworking may not be for you. But if what I've described so far has piqued your interest, here are some of the potential benefits:

- **They boost creativity and productivity**

  No more corporate, boring, bland office walls. Most coworking spaces are effectively set up to look and feel playful. Working in these surroundings *feels nice.* Of course, this is going to have a tremendous effect on how creative you are.

- **You meet new contacts, and friends**

  Because socialising isn't compulsory or forced (my pet hate), you are able to meet new people with ease, without the unnecessary feeling that work politics may get in the way. Everyone is their own boss, and this means you hang out with people because you genuinely like them, not because you feel you have to. You'll get more authentic connections as a result, and even meet people who can help your business.

- **You can access the space when you're most productive**

  A lot of coworking spaces operate outside the normal

9-5. So if you've spent a day at the beach, and it's 7pm, and you're fired up for a good 6 hours of work, you can access your coworking space.

- **Reduce business costs**

  Although you pay a fee for a coworking space, you don't have to worry about the standard utility bills that come with renting an office or working at home. All of your heating, lighting and electricity is taken care of, and usually quite a few other things, too. Most coworking spaces offer free refreshments and access to meeting rooms, conference call facilities, and ultra-fast wifi connections.

Beautiful coworking spaces

When I think about it, the inspiration for being a freedom seeker, and probably the motivation for writing this book, was when I visited Hubud (www.hubud.org) in 2016.

Hubud is a coworking space in Ubud, Bali, and having been in stuffy, depressing offices most of my life, I was literally blown away at this space. It is made of bamboo, and offers a cafe, hammocks in the garden, beautiful open air scenery as you work overlooking lush green rice fields. You have to take your shoes off at the door as you go in, and this creates a really relaxed working vibe.

It was more than just the look of the place, though. It was the *feeling* I got when I was there. I watched people from all over the globe laughing, chatting, interacting, hugging each other, and I thought 'wow, this really is the future.' These spaces are transforming us as well as our work.

Here's a few more of the 'must see' ones, although there are now literally hundreds if not thousands, in the world. You'll be able to find one in your city, I'm sure.

We Work

We Work has offices all over the world; and has recently been valued at $20 billion, which is no doubt proof that this trend is on the rise. They also have a sister company, We Live, which is their coliving section of the business. We work (www.wework.com) offices are in many different countries around the world; including the US, Brazil, Japan, China and India, but we love the London ones - there are nineteen so far, with more to be built.

The spaces are gorgeously designed and most have a games room on offer, phone booths, an outdoor terrace or garden for lunchtime meetings or yoga. You'll also get free fruit water, freshly brewed coffee, and beer on tap, should you wish to indulge.

Kohub

KoHub (www.kohub.org) describes itself as a 'tropical coworking space', and it is indeed just that. Based in Ko Lanta, Thailand, it offers a 'family environment', and is a great place to hang out, work, and meet some interesting people.

It's a two minute walk to the beach; but there's rest and relaxation at the hub if you want it. With a lush tropical garden with hammocks, a courtyard and a full restaurant and juice bar, you probably won't want to leave your office at the end of the day - now who can say that?

With free coffee, tea and one of the fastest wifi speeds in Thailand, it's no surprise that KoHub is on the list of travelling digital nomads.

Impact Hub

There are several IMPACT (www.impacthub.net) hubs all over the world; 81 to be exact. There are also 21 in progress, so in the next year or so (by 2018), expect 100 of these all over the world.

Second Home - Second home (www.secondhome.io) is located next to TimeOut Market in Lisbon, and it's fast becoming one of the coolest coworking spaces there are. With a library, a green 'wellbeing space', yoga sessions and a running club, there's plenty of opportunities to get involved with their member community. There are also several Second Home spaces in London if you fancy trying one on UK soil.

Home

Of course, you can work in your own home. This has it's many benefits, and once you know what works for you, you'll be able to decide if it's right.

Pro's include: eating your own food (not popping to the shop or eating out), being in your own surroundings, being able to do chores, oh and totally working naked should you wish to (mind that hot laptop ;)).

The cons include: being in your own surroundings, being isolated, and being distracted.

You'll notice that being in your own surroundings is both a pro and a con. If you don't mind using your home space as your work space, then maybe it's not a big deal, but for me personally, I find that my best work never comes when I'm at home. For others, they may love being able to 'Netflix and chill' whilst they're writing a few articles or designing a powerpoint. It's gotta work for you.

The companies leading the way

You don't have to go it alone, you know. There are some companies out there who truly get this, and want you to be your very best self.

Buffer (www.buffer.com) is one of them. Buffer were pioneers in the remote work industry, and even penned a book, 'Better Remote Work'. They are keen to understand what makes human productivity thrive; and it is for this reason they adopt a holistic approach to work and work-life balance.

The Smarter Working Initiative (www.smarterworkinginitiative. com) is a new initiative that aims to encourage employers to promote flexible working within their organisation.

Software development company Articulate (www.articulate. com) creates tools to author e-learning courses. All of their staff work remotely, and they organise annual company retreats.

Keep checking the various sites for companies that will allow you to be based from anywhere. I always do a search on Indeed.com for 'Remote Work' or 'Home Based.'

Success in remote work

Productivity hacks

Now I was just going to title this section 'productivity', but I figured, everyone needs a hack in their life, right?

Having no physical boss in your life is super for many reasons, especially if you like being autonomous. But if you're the type of person that can easily fall into a Youtube cat hole (or other forms of online videos!) we need to have a serious chat.

At the end of the day, no one wants the freedom seeking lifestyle as much as you, right? You gotta be your own boss, which means from time to time you've got to crack the whip on yourself.

Here's some little tips to help you be the master boss of your own life:

- **Find out where you are most productive**

  This is especially important if you do a creative pursuit, such as writing or thinking of concepts. It's pretty darn difficult to get fired up when you are in an uninspiring place.

- **Surround yourself with the right people**

If you are around lazy energy, with people who are just drifting along in their lives, it's not exactly going to help you, unless you make a concerted effort to be different from them. It's vital that you are around people that uplift and inspire you; as these people will fuel you with the energy to succeed.

- **Maintain an optimistic, yet realistic attitude**

Rome wasn't built in a day. So don't beat yourself up if the company you started six months ago isn't letting you travel the world three times over already. Make no bones about it, this life is TOUGH! You have to put the work in. And sometimes, you will work your little ass off. Other days, you will struggle to lift a finger. Don't beat yourself up about it; that's just how life is.

- **Use tools to keep you focused**

Heard of Rescue Time? This productivity hack monitors your online activity, and will tell you how much you really spend on Twitter or Facebook. It is a good indicator of how much time you actually spend working, and if you're a person who loses focus easily like me, you can use it to better structure your work day - perhaps breaking it up into short chunks rather than a full day.

- **Learn and manage your energy**

This is all about knowing how you work best, and including both action and non-action into your working day. There's lots of evidence out there to suggest that a full on eight or nine hour day with just one break isn't actually the best solution. Users were found to be more productive when they scheduled in more 'rest breaks' throughout the day.

Your work toolbox

As we know, the digital landscape is changing all the time, and in writing this book I knew much of it will become obsolete within a few years. Oh well! As one of my all time inspirations, Martin Luther King says *"Even if I knew that tomorrow the world would go to pieces, I would still plant my apple tree."*

Here's a list of some of the best tools I currently use when working remotely:

Harvest: (www.getharvest.com) A free time-tracking software tool. The free version only lets you have two projects, but it's pretty good, especially if you are on a retainer with clients, if you're a freelancer. Even if you work on a project basis, it's interesting to see how long things are taking you.

Slack: (www.slack.com) The all around fabulous real-time chat tool.

Pexels: (www.pexels.com) A really beautiful royalty-free image site!

Canva: (www.canva.com) My life has transformed with Canva! It's really amazing. It's a free design tool that lets you create amazing designs for logos, social media posts, presentations, cover images, pretty much everything (guess who designed this book cover, and how?)

Momentum: (search in Chrome app store) I love this app from Chrome. Really pretty pictures, nice inspirational quotes, and a little to do list, which is good for either using as a daily task list or a 'musn't forget!' list, which I use it for.

<u>Freeagent</u>: (www.freeagent.com) A great tool for invoicing, although you do have to pay for it.

<u>Adparlour</u>: **(**www.adparlour.com) A great little tool for checking Facebook ads, you can drop your copy and picture in and it will show up exactly how it does on Facebook.

<u>Trello:</u> (www.trello.com) I love Trello. It's a great little app for sorting your life and work into categories. You can have many 'boards' (topics), and then lots of 'cards', which act like lists for you to check tasks off.

Working with other people remotely

> *'Trust is the glue of life. It's the most essential ingredient in effective communication. It's the foundational principle that holds all relationships' - Stephen Covey*

Unless you use a constant video presence, chances are that the people you work with aren't going to be visible to you on a regular basis - you're not always going to be able to see what they are doing.

This brings up two essential elements in a working relationship that almost become more important when you work remotely:

Trust;
And
Communication.

Of course, you can't really have one without the other - you won't trust a worker that doesn't communicate very much!

When you first start working with someone, whether it's a freelancer or remote work boss, it's crucial you establish trust from the outset. Without non-verbal cues and your presence around them, they have to know that not only will you do the work, but you are aligned to the needs of their business.

So how do you do that? Well, the most important element of a successful remote working career is the ability to build and nurture the relationships with people. This will then naturally build trust. You don't know them, you may never get the chance to meet them, so how do you build a relationship?

- **Be visible**

Being visible means being available. If you've got a Slack channel that you use for work, or Skype, don't make yourself invisible or sign off. Ensure that for the time you're working, you're around. If you may not be available for a certain amount of time, let people know.

- **Be positive**

Your boss or freelance client can't hear your chirpy voice on an email, so it's vitally important you get this right. In my early twenties, I was told my emails were 'too blunt', and I spent years mastering the art of a really positive email. Make sure you are phrasing things in a positive manner, even if it's something that is difficult or challenging. You can't erase a rude email.

- **Be transparent**

This means being upfront about how long things will take. Remote work can be great for you speedy gonzales workers out there; you'll get more done and be able to finish up earlier.

Some online work sites uses a screenshot tool to track your work, but if that isn't available to you, always give a realistic timeframe - don't put too much pressure on yourself to deliver.

- **Communicate regularly**

Being in communication builds the relationship as it shows you can be trusted, and you're on the ball. Even short emails such as confirming receipt of an email, or letting a client know when you'll deliver the work can make all the difference.

Spotting a 'shark'

Unfortunately, in the world of remote work there are some unscrupulous people. They hide behind their laptop millions of miles away, want to work with you and then disappear without a trace, leaving you frustrated, annoyed and (sometimes) out of pocket.

With certain types of jobs you just have to go with your gut instinct. If they are demanding too much of you upfront (*'Hey, could you write a 500 word article as an unpaid trial?'*) or not outlining the work clearly, something is wrong. You will get a sense of 'hey, isn't this too good to be true?'

You can spot a 'shark' by the way they *don't do* everything listed above. They're not transparent, they don't communicate regularly (or they are erratic in their communication), and they are often hard to get hold of. Therefore, they erode trust early on and leave you wondering what the hell just happened.

There are many ways to avoid getting duped:

- **Establish a very clear brief or contract of employment**

Make sure you know exactly what you are signing up for and the scope of work. If you have any questions, outline these in writing before you begin. This is crucial because it shows the other party you're not just walking in blindly to the relationship. You know what you're aiming to deliver, by what date, and you outline the compensation for the services provided.

- **Save copies of the work you produce**

This seems obvious, but is especially true if you are working collaboratively on a document such as Google Drive. Downloading a separate copy means you will have a spare to hand should you need it. If you work on 'live' documents, they can easily get deleted or modified by collaborators, so ensure you save backups.

- **Give them a couple of opportunities to fail**

Everyone makes mistakes, but repeated ones (like disappearing for days or not paying you on time) should ring alarm bells. If you've given someone the benefit of the doubt for a few days but they are still disrespecting your relationship, then maybe it's time to call it a day.

Maintaining your freedom

Keeping healthy - the foundation for being free

There is a certain risk to managing your own time, career, and money, because it means that your health becomes even more important.

If you're sick, you're not free. You can't travel. You can't do all of those wonderful things on your bucket list, because all your energy is spent on making yourself better.

If you're sick, you risk your security. Not just money - but you risk your creativity, your social life, and all the other great things that comes from being a wonderful, flourishing human being.

Keeping healthy is the foundation for being free.

And I'm not just talking about physical health.

Health is a combination of mental, spiritual, physical and emotional wellbeing, and it's important to define your idea of 'healthy' before you dive into a more freedom based lifestyle, because if you don't define what a healthy life is for you before you start, the more likely it is you may fall into a trap.

For example, if you haven't defined what healthy looks like in your emotional sphere, you may find yourself simply taking on too much work, and struggling to say no to work that comes your way. This feeling of obligation leads you to become stressed, and then you're more likely to also suffer physical ailments, as well as being drained emotionally.

The way I see it, health (in a holistic sense) = happiness = freedom.

You can't be truly free if you're not happy, right? You're in a prison of your own doing, you're creating miserable circumstances for your life without realising.

So by defining what health looks like for you at all levels, you are setting up a life that not only ensures your happiness, but ensures your freedom too.

Make a note of what healthy looks like to you on all levels, so that you can keep your life in balance even after you've started your Freedom Seeking Path.

I feel mentally healthy when I

____

____

____

____

I feel emotionally healthy when I

____

____

____

____

I feel physically healthy when I

____

____

____

____

I feel spiritually healthy when I

____

____

____

____

Being a minimalist

Being a minimalist seems to be all the rage at the moment. Ever seen the gameshow 'The Cube?' Minimalism is essentially about putting a 'simplify' on your life. But why is it useful for a freer lifestyle?

Well, it allows you to free up your finances to concentrate on the things in life that are important to you. If you're not shopping, you may or may not have freed up a valuable part of your weekend.

My cousin is a minimalist, although he probably wouldn't define himself in those terms. He dresses simply, lives in a shared house, and doesn't spend extravagantly. His highest goal is financial freedom, and it is because of this he has managed to save nearly £100,000 in cash, ready to buy a small house outright. He isn't from a wealthy background; quite the opposite, he grew up on a council estate. But he has managed to simplify his life so much that he is a freer person.

Minimalism can help when you're travelling, too. Many people who adopt a minimalistic approach to their wardrobe have adopted the idea of a 'capsule wardrobe'; those pieces you love and will wear time and time again. In this way, you can invest in good quality pieces that will not only last the test of time, but will look stylish.

Minimalism is essentially a 'cut the crap' approach. It's not about eating endless beans on toast sat in a sparse flat, wearing a black t-shirt and jeans. It's about getting rid of the stuff that weighs you down.

We often forget that sometimes a key to feeling lighter and freer is by simply getting rid of stuff. That doesn't just mean physical objects; it means removing habits that may be a massive drain on your time.

For example, I don't really enjoy food shopping. It is laborious, and to be honest, if I'm hungry, I'll buy more. I don't like fighting through aisles of people in a trance, all looking for stuff to buy. I can spend up to an hour or more doing a big shop in a supermarket, and I'd rather not. So I buy my food online, and save my shopping lists. Any fresh fruit or veg I need I get, but I can always pick up extras should I need to.

My shopping takes around 20 minutes to do, I can browse thousands of items with a simple search. I then spend my free time going for a long walks and getting out in the open air!

You can simplify your life in almost any way.

Here's a few ways to get you started…

What activities use up my spare time most?

____

____

____

Is there a way I could simplify these?

____

____

____

What stuff do I have, but not really need?

____

____

____

Where do I waste time', and how can I stop it?

____

____

____

Creating an iron will

My late grandad always used to go on about remembering 'Percy'. 'What are you talking about Grandad?' I'd say. 'Percy Verance' he would say.

Remembering perseverance and remembering to be disciplined are the two main lessons my grandad passed to me, and whilst I found them incredibly boring as a teenager I now realise the value of them. If you want to get anywhere in life, you have to develop the strength of character to see yourself through tough times.

On a recent holiday, my friend was reading Switch: How to

change things when change is hard. We were chatting about how difficult I find things, and I have a tendency to give up when the going gets tough. She mentioned how the book explains the theory and process of change, and how our minds can be resistant to it. (This has helped me a lot when writing this book, as even though it's a small book, it's been a pain in the arse to write!)

Most of the time, creating any sort of change in our lives involves removing subconscious blocks or beliefs about the thing it is that we are seeking. When things are not going so well, we tend to quit rather than looking at where we are unconsciously self-sabotaging.

The best way to overcome these and develop an iron will, is to know what your values are. If you don't know what you truly value in life, you'll either end up feeling a) incredibly conflicted and/or b) like the struggle just ain't worth it.

There were so many times I came close to leading a freedom based lifestyle, but then things would get financially tough, and I would panic. I would then go back into an ordinary office job, and within a matter of months I would feel stuck and frustrated, knowing I had so much more to give, but lacking the energy, motivation and belief to do anything about it. This cycle continued for years. It went something like this

'Yay! I've quit! Hello freedom!'
(Starts to gain small successes towards the life I wanted)
'Oh wow, this is actually happening, I can do this!'
(Small successes plateau or fade away, have a quiet period)
'Uh-oh, turns out things aren't working out so well. Maybe I shouldn't have quit?'
(worry and panic continues)
'I need to get a job; I'm going to lose all my money!

(gets a job)

I found it incredibly easy to get a normal office job; I was very fortunate in that regard. But I didn't realise my highest value was freedom.

I have a Henry David Thoreau card in my kitchen. It is a bird with it's wings attached by strings, and the quote says **'All good things are wild and free'.** I believe this to be true. Freedom should be the foundation for your life, as long as you are not intentionally hurting anyone else.

I believe true love is freedom. When you love something, you allow it to be free. You allow it to be what it is, without trying to change or control it. It is an acceptance, and in order for us to become free ourselves we need to know that we are worthy.

The best way to find out what your values are is to find out what's important to you.

From there, you can develop an iron will by sticking to your choice, knowing that you're aligning yourself to your highest values. The road may not be easy; but it will be worth it.

_______________________________ is important to me in work

_______________________________ is important to me in work

_______________________________ is important to me in work

_______________________________ is important to me in work

_______________________________ is important to me in a relationship

_______________________________ is important to me in a relationship

__________________________________ is important to me in a relationship

__________________________________ is important to me in a relationship

__________________________________ is important to me in general

__________________________________ is important to me in general

__________________________________ is important to me in general

__________________________________ is important to me in general

Don't worry if you can't think of something for every category. If you're struggling to think of something, remember a time when you really enjoyed a situation, or really disliked it. What in there wasn't right for you?

This will help you figure out most important. In a career, is it creativity, money, freedom, collaboration with others, recognition, respect, a sense of purpose?

In a relationship is it trust, honesty, friendship, laughter, chemistry, meaning or kindness?

Of course, all values are important to us as human beings, but some we will value more than others. Once you figure out what's truly important to you and why (what this will mean for you), then it will be easier to commit to action, as you have the right motivation in mind.

Meditation

Now you may think it strange for me to include a chapter about meditation in this book, but the effects it has had on my life are so profound, that I couldn't not include it.

Meditation can help you become a freedom seeker in a different way. When the Buddha was asked 'What have you gained from meditation? He said 'Nothing! However, let me tell you what I have lost. I have lost: anger, anxiety, depression, insecurity, fear of old age and death'.

I had dabbled in meditation throughout my life, but never really committed to a steady practice until my thirties.

I've realised it's only when you commit to an ongoing practice do you see results in your life. For example, you don't go to the gym and expect to get ripped in a few days, do you?

When you are meditating, it's the equivalent of getting mentally strong. Do you know why?

Because within each of us is an endless source of deep peace. A peace so beautiful, that if we accessed it on a daily basis, we'd all be a lot happier.

It's not easy when you start meditating, because your mind jumps all over the place. Just stick with it. I imagine my breath as a source of light, entering and leaving my body. I don't count or anything like that. When I find my thoughts pulling me away, I simply go back to breathing the light. No judgement, no beating myself up. It's a process.

I think the reason why a lot of us have such difficulty meditating is because our minds are running much faster than meditation allows. To really get to the deep still point in meditation, you have to be extremely still in your consciousness, and of course modern life rarely allows for that.

It's like there's a well within you, and at first you can only access the top of the well, which doesn't really feel very different, but the more times you meditate, the deeper down the well you go, until you reach near the bottom, and then your experience suddenly becomes a whole lot different. It's like you're learning to deep dive in the ocean of your own mind.

This is why I believe being a Freedom Seeker allows people more access to the benefits of meditation. They can meditate easily without worrying that they have to get back to work, or that they have to leave the house.

Imagine what the world would be like if more people meditated. This is what I hope comes from a more freedom based lifestyle; where we look up from our striving and struggling and running towards our goals. It is about fully living in the present, and celebrating the journey each and every day.

Even if you have kids, it's easy to meditate. Wait until they're in bed asleep, or meditate in the morning. Just 20 minutes a day is absolutely fine. Get comfy, put a timer on your phone, and breathe. It will get easier each day - just see it as your little 'me time', that you need every day, rather than a meditation.

My thoughts about meditation:

____

____

____

____

____

Finding your place

Every ship needs an anchor; and whilst you could in theory

travel the world many many times until you die; most people need some kind of 'down time' and a rest from all of that gallivanting.

I've lived in lots of places throughout my life; I've lived in about 20 different houses in my life, and have lived in 4 different cities in the UK.

Being on the move allows you to be flexible and adaptable; you find it easy to speak to new people, and you learn ways of integrating into a given society wherever you are.

I have put down some roots in my hometown of Nottingham; practically, it makes sense for me to do so here, as I am close to people. I am also frequently in Manchester; a place that shaped me who I am today and where I consider my 'spiritual home.'

I meet in the middle by going for walks with friends in the Peak District; I enjoy the hectic pace and bustle of Manchester nightlife, but also enjoy the relative ruralness of places I've lived, with horses across the road and a chicken in my backyard.

I would encourage anyone to go to a new city and test out living there; even if it's just for a few weeks. If you go alone, you'll really get out of your comfort zone and it will stretch you in ways you never thought possible.

Living a freedom based lifestyle is about broadening your horizons, and realising we don't have to do things in one place. Mix it up. I have stayed in airbnbs in my own city to get a change of mindset and have some personal time and space. Sometimes it's just about changing the little things, in order to make a difference to how free you feel.

When you work remotely, finding your place becomes easier. You want to live on a farm in rural Scotland? With wifi, you can! You want to work from a yacht in the Med? Go do it! With remote work, the whole world can be your home.

You're not tied to your hometown - the world is your oyster. You can stay in these places for longer than a week or two, and really allow their culture to seep into your being.

5 places I would like to explore in more depth:

1. ____

2. ____

3. ____

4. ____

5. ____

Finding your people

> *'One of the most beautiful qualities of true friendship is to understand and be understood'*
> *- Seneca*

The world is more connected than ever before; yet in some ways it feels like we are more disconnected than ever before.

Social media and the advent of digital technology has meant we can have very transient relationships. As more of us continue to move across the globe, we keep in touch with the growing numbers of people we meet via a Facebook post, an Instagram Update, a Snapchat or a Whatsapp.

We have become media publishers; and the fact that our lives are so full, and that we can travel so often means that we can often miss out on deep, rich relationships.

We can flow from one thing to the next, travelling to different countries, but lacking that deep, soulful connection that arises from trusting another, going through hardships, and

Apart from your partner, when did you last really *connect* with another human being? I don't just mean a catch up at a coffee shop, I mean really connect - share a transformative experience together?

Freedom seekers know that connecting with other humans is the reason they do what they do. Sure, it's sun, money, increased time and energy, but none of that would mean anything if it all took place within a vacuum.

At the end of our lives, it's those memories with others that mean the most to us.

I'm a bit of a closet anthropologist; I'm always studying other human beings and trying to identify trends in our evolution from the people that I speak to. I find it absolutely fascinating what is happening on our planet today, and I can say with 100% certainty that humans have a deep need for community and connection. From my own experience, I know that without it, life can not only be more difficult, but your health suffers as a result.

Imagine your life as a thread, connecting to all the people you know around the world.

Why are these people in your life?
What is it about them that you love being around?

How can you get more of this 'good stuff' as a Freedom Seeker?

Leaving aside the notion of family for a second, I want to discuss the topic of friends as a Freedom Seeker.

You're likely to have friends in different countries; or be friends with people who are constantly jetting off. All of my very best friends have a passion for travel and new experiences; they're always going to broaden their horizons in some way or another. That means we are often like passing ships; but when we do meet, there's inevitably a huge burst of energy and enthusiasm between us.

There's so much talk these days about 'finding your tribe'. It's a bit of a cliche now that phrase, but what it's really about is about finding people that understand you and *get* you.

Think about when you were at your happiest. What were you doing? What interests did you have?

Here's the deal: when you're buzzing off some activity or hobby you're doing, you are 'lit up'. That energy and radiance affects other people, and makes you magnetic and easy to talk to.

Finding your path

There are over 7 billion of us on this beautiful planet. What fascinates me is culture, and how cultural norms are so ingrained into our mindsets.

Cultural norms are the gridlines that most people take in a given society because it's the 'done thing.' If you're in a particular culture but decide that you want to take a different life path, it can be difficult.

Let me share some examples:

- Being in an arranged marriage culture but being gay

- Living in a family business where you're expected to carry it on, but you don't enjoy it

- Feeling pressured to buy a house but you are keen to keep travelling

- Wanting to live in a community but feeling isolated

- Having people laugh at you because you homeschool your children

As individual as we are, we are all unique. We can't follow some cookie-cutter prescribed way of being.

Travelling can open your eyes to new cultures and ways of being. It makes you realise that the cultural norms we follow are usually imposed upon ourselves. It takes an immense amount of courage to not follow these 'unwritten rules', but the fact is we *can*, and people *do*.

It may mean changing your life circumstances, but if you understand yourself and what makes you happy, then it's easier to make the leap.

I've moved around quite a lot in my life, and met lots of different people from different cultures. I never wanted to live an ordinary 'suburban' life, the thought of it bored the hell out of me.

When I moved back to my hometown of Nottingham I felt

incredibly, incredibly alone. It seemed like literally everyone was playing a game that I just didn't enjoy, and was supposed to. I started to internalise a feeling of 'what's wrong with me?' and literally forced myself to pretend to be conventional for four years, trying to fit into the mould, but all the while feeling a deep sense of disappointment.

I finally got the courage to break free of the pressure I put on myself to have a 'normal' life, relationship, and career, and it was probably one of the hardest things I have ever done. When you know people will judge you negatively for making a certain decision or taking some action, it requires an incredible amount of self trust and self respect to do the brave thing. The reason why it took me so long is because I desperately wanted these people's love, approval, and understanding. I thought that if I honoured myself, I would not get that, and it really hurt me to admit it. I'm quite a spiritually sensitive person, so even if they never said anything to me about how they felt, I would feel their judgements on an emotional level.

I realised that I had to come to a place within myself that honoured unconditional love, not conditional, and realised that if I was making choices in my life out of fear or of the worry of other people not loving me then I was indeed in a prison of my own making.

That's why I wrote this book.

How to talk to people that don't 'get it'

> *'People think you're crazy if you talk about things they don't understand' - Elvis Presley*

Make no bones about it, this kind of lifestyle is *new*.

This means that people may find it difficult to understand where you're coming from. It could be your parents, it could be people in your current job, it could even be your friends and your partner.

The future of work is going to look very, very different than spending forty years of your life in a factory, or staying with one or two jobs throughout your lifetime.

Firstly, remember that for people that have been born into a different era, remote working is unchartered territory. They don't know anything about it. They will have fears, concerns, and questions.

The best way to alleviate fears about anything is to become knowledgeable. If you're certain that this is the path you want to take, read up on it. That way you'll be able to face your own fears, concerns and questions before you meet them in others.

If you're still unsure, the best approach is to keep very quiet about your freedom seeking plans, until you have established a clear plan of action, and have the necessary faith and determination to see it through.

Otherwise, your plans will be foiled with the lightest of comments and the smallest of setbacks. It's important that *you* are comfortable with your decision before you share it with anyone else.

If you really need to share your plans, make sure you are remembering the following:

This is all new to them: They have no idea what this new life may look like for you. Share examples of those who have been there, done that, so they can see that it's actually possible.

Answer the fears they may have: Draw up a calculation of how much money you need to leave your job, or make a note of your earning potential whilst in a remote career. If they can see you've done the groundwork, it won't feel so scary to them.

Share evidence from the mainstream media: There are lots of news articles, thought pieces and programmes on the future of work. By mentioning these, you're showing that you are jumping onto a growing trend, and this is how the world of work is transforming.

Have a backup plan: If you have a plan B, then plan A doesn't seem so scary. By backing up your ideas with an alternative plan, it becomes much less risky for yourself and the people around you.

The proof is in the pudding; and whilst your loved ones may not be supportive of you now, they will come round to the idea once you're living your life in the way you've designed and are ultimately happier as a result.

Freedom seekers: the choice is up to you

> *'A golden cage is still just a cage.' - Anita Krizzman*

Whether you want to live a freer life physically or mentally, it all starts with you. We all need that precious balance of freedom and safety; and recognising where your comfort zones are and where you'd like them to be is ultimately down to you.

No-one can tell you how to live your life; there isn't a rulebook for doing things. What society, or your friends, or your parents think is the right way, might not be necessarily the right way for you.

You have to find your flow. And whatever that looks like to others, it doesn't matter as long as you are buzzing and thriving from it. A happy, healthy, energetic person is going to do far more for the world than one who is lost and miserable.

It's time to shift things up a gear.

I'll leave you with a few steps... the rest is up to you.

- Start with clearing out the clutter - and I don't just mean what you own.

- Clear out the toxic thoughts, those oughts and shoulds. Chuck them in a bin bag, and replace them with positive, inspirational messages.

- Remove physical objects from your space - take bits to a charity shop, lighten your load.

- Learn what makes you feel bad about yourself, and take steps to stop doing it.

- Remember just because everyone else is doing it, doesn't mean you have to.

- Your path is your path, their path is theirs.

- Enjoy your small freedoms, because these matter.

- Ask yourself what makes you come alive, and have the courage to build your life around the answer.

Enjoy the ride.

____

104

Disclaimer: All links in this book and mentions are either companies I have personally used or have heard of via a recommendation.

9 781975 708634